THE CIRCULATORY SYSTEM

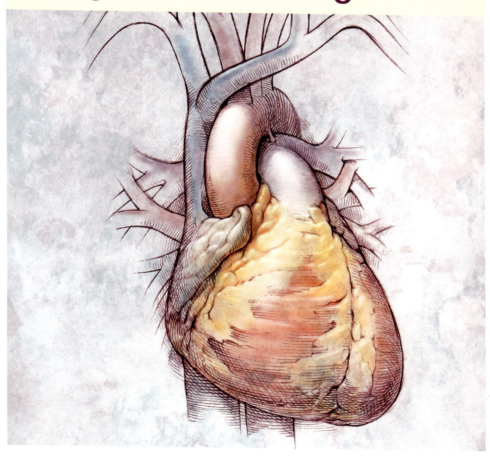

By Susan H. Gray

The Child's World

Published in the United States of America by the Child's World®
P.O. Box 326, Chanhassen, MN 55317-0326
800-599-READ
www.childsworld.com

Photo Credits: Cover: Artville/ ScottBodell; Bettmann/Corbis: 17; Corbis: 4 (Duomo), 6 (Howard Sochureck), 10 (Jim Zuckerman), 12 (Ronnie Kaufman), 16 (Hulton-Deutsch Collection), 25, 27 (Ariel Skelley); Custom Medical Stock Pictures: 9, 13, 14, 15, 18, 19, 20, 22, 24; Photo Edit: 7 (Rudy Von Briel), 26 (Mark Richards).

The Child's World®: Mary Berendes, Publishing Director

Editorial Directions, Inc.: E. Russell Primm, Editorial Director; Elizabeth K. Martin, Line Editor; Katie Marsico, Assistant Editor; Olivia Nellums, Editorial Assistant; Susan Hindman, Copy Editor; Elizabeth K. Martin, Proofreader; Peter Garnham, Marilyn Mallin, Mary Hoffman, Fact Checkers; Tim Griffin/IndexServ, Indexer; Cian Loughlin O'Day, Photo Researcher; Linda S. Koutris, Photo Selector

Library of Congress Cataloging-in-Publication Data
Gray, Susan Heinrichs.
 The circulatory system / by Susan H. Gray.
    p. cm. — (Living well)
Includes bibliographical references and index.
Contents: What is the circulatory system?—What is blood?—What happens in the heart?—Where does blood go next?—What happens in the lungs?
 ISBN 1-59296-036-7 (lib. bdg. : alk. paper)
 1. Cardiovascular system—Juvenile literature. [1. Circulatory system.] I. Title. II. Series: Living well (Child's World (Firm)
 QP103.G73 2004
 612.1—dc21   2003006288

Subject adviser:
R. John Solaro, Ph.D.,
Distinguished
University Professor
and Head, Department
of Physiology and
Biophysics, University
of Illinois Chicago,
Chicago, Illinois

TABLE OF CONTENTS

CHAPTER ONE

NATHAN'S RACE

Nathan was up for this race. He had practiced running all year long. Today, his whole school was cheering him on. Nathan and boys from five other schools were in

As Nathan waited at the starting block, his circulatory system was already at work, pumping blood all over his body.

the starting blocks. Not one of them said a word. They were all thinking about the race.

Suddenly, the official fired his pistol. The boys shot forward and raced down the track. As Nathan ran, his muscles worked harder and harder. He sucked in air faster and faster. Oxygen (OX-ih-jen) gas from the air went into every space in his lungs. It moved into blood passing near those spaces. The oxygen-filled blood went right to his heart.

Nathan's heart was pounding. With each beat, it pushed oxygen-rich blood out to the rest of his body. Blood went to his legs as they ran. Blood flowed to his arms as they pumped back and forth. Blood rushed to his chest muscles as they heaved in and out. Wherever the blood went, it brought oxygen and **nutrients.** Nathan's body tissues **absorbed** them so they could keep working.

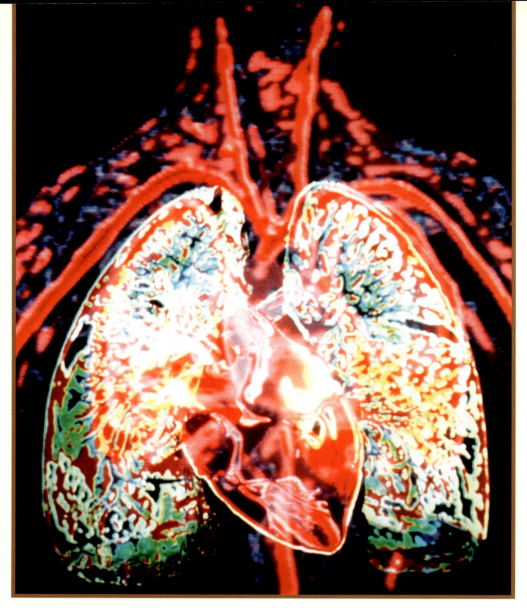

A digital scan of Nathan's chest, like this one, would show his heart and lungs working together to bring oxygen to every part of his body.

As the tissues used the oxygen and nutrients, they made a gas

called carbon dioxide (dy-OX-ide). Blood took the gas and hauled it

away from the tissues. Loaded with carbon dioxide, Nathan's blood moved back to his heart. The heart sent the blood to his lungs again.

There, carbon dioxide left Nathan's body, and more oxygen came in.

And it all happened in just a few seconds.

Nathan could see the finish line now. His legs were moving so fast they were a blur. Blood vessels in his neck were bulging. Nathan was gasping for air. He crossed the line just barely ahead of the other boys. His circulatory (SUR-kyoo-luh-tore-ee) system had pulled him through.

Nathan's circulatory system gave his body the oxygen and nutrients it needed to win the race.

CHAPTER TWO

WHAT IS THE CIRCULATORY SYSTEM?

The circulatory system moves blood to and from every part of the body. This system includes the blood, the heart, and all of the blood vessels. To circulate (SUR-kyoo-late) means to move around in a circle. Blood does not exactly make a circle as it flows through the body. But as it moves, it keeps coming back through the heart.

The heart is the organ that pumps blood throughout the body. Inside, it has four sections, or chambers. Two chambers are in the top and two are in the bottom. Each top chamber is called an atrium (AY-tree-um). Each bottom chamber is called a ventricle (VEN-trik-ul). The heart has a right atrium and right ventricle. On the other side, it has a left atrium and left ventricle.

Each time the heart beats, it squeezes and forces blood out. Blood flows around the rest of the body through blood vessels. There are three kinds of blood vessels. They are the arteries (AR-tur-eez), the veins (VANES), and the capillaries (KAP-uh-lehr-eez).

The heart pumps blood throughout the body through arteries, shown here in red, veins, shown in blue, and capillaries, which connect the veins and arteries.

Blood flowing away from the heart moves through arteries. Arteries have muscular, **elastic** walls. The walls of the main arteries pulse, or throb, each time the heart beats. When you feel a pulse in your wrist or neck, you are feeling the throb of an artery. Arteries do

The walls of an artery, such as the one above, are muscular and elastic.

not beat on their own. They throb because of the blood surging through them.

As arteries get farther from the heart, they split up into smaller and smaller vessels. The vessels finally become so small they can be seen only with a microscope. These vessels are called capillaries.

After flowing through the capillaries, blood starts moving back to the heart. The tiny capillaries begin to come together. They join to form larger vessels. These vessels are called veins. They carry blood back to the heart. Vein walls are not as thick and muscular as those of arteries. And veins do not throb with each heartbeat. The inner walls of many veins have little flaps in them called valves. The valves come together to stop blood from moving backward. This keeps blood flowing toward the heart.

Human beings have a circulatory system that is closed. No matter where blood moves in the body, it always stays enclosed in the system. Birds, fish, and reptiles also have closed systems.

Spiders and insects have a circulatory system that is very different. They have an open system. Blood passes through the heart and is pumped out. It then moves through a large vessel or vessels with an open end. Blood spills from the vessel freely and washes over all the organs. Tissues take up nutrients as the blood flows by. The animal's normal movements push blood back toward the heart.

CHAPTER THREE

WHAT IS BLOOD?

Blood is a fluid that contains many different materials.

One of the materials is plasma (PLAZ-muh). It is a liquid that is the color of straw. Plasma is made up mainly of water. It carries nutrients, red and white blood cells, and platelets throughout the body.

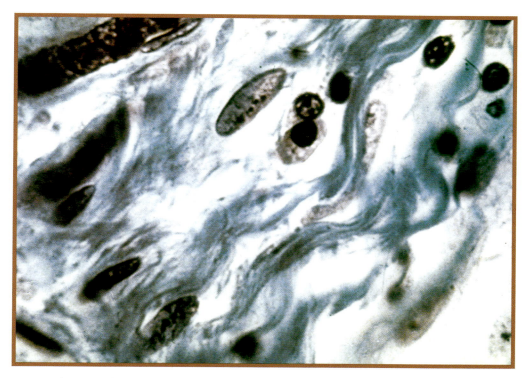

Plasma is the material in blood that carries nutrients, blood cells, and platelets.

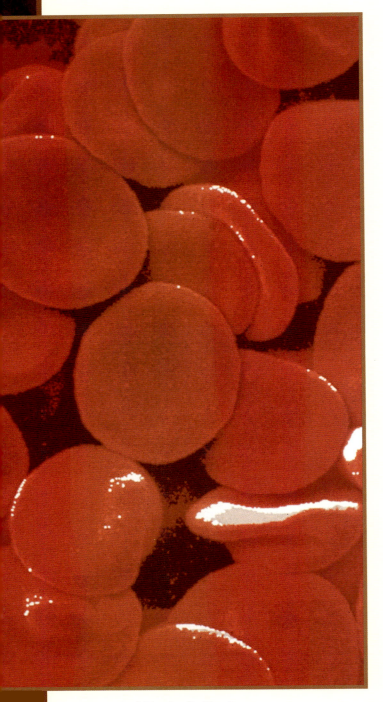

Red blood cells like these carry oxygen all over the body.

Most cells in the blood are red cells. A red blood cell looks like a ball that is squashed in the middle. Red cells carry oxygen to all the other cells in the body.

There are many fewer white blood cells than red ones. But white blood cells have a very important job. They defend the body against germs that cause **infection.** White cells recognize germs that do not belong in the body. In some cases, they stick right to the germ and begin destroying it. In other cases, they produce chemicals to attack the germ.

Blood also contains tiny platelets. They help the blood to clot, or harden, when bleeding occurs. When a person gets a cut or scrape, platelets near the injury stick together. They form a little clump. The clump dries and becomes a scab.

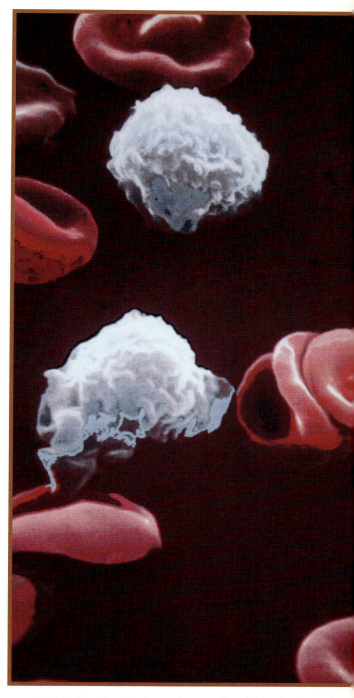

White blood cells, shown here with red blood cells, help keep the body healthy.

Queen Victoria ruled Great Britain for much of the 1800s. She and her husband, Prince Albert, had nine children (pictured below). Their family life was busy and happy. One thing, though, brought them much sadness.

Their little son Leopold had a terrible blood disease called hemophilia (HEE-mo-FILL-ee-uh). When people with this disease begin to bleed, their blood does not clot.

People with hemophilia can bleed to death from a simple cut.

Boys get the disease much more often than girls do. However, girls are often "carriers." This means they do not have hemophilia themselves. But their sons may get the disease and their daughters may be carriers.

Two of the queen's daughters were carriers and did not know it. They married members of other

royal families in Europe and had children of their own. Sickly little Leopold also grew up and started a family. In these families, some of the children had hemophilia and some were carriers. The disease was passed down from generation to generation. Over the years, it spread to other royal families. Royal couples in Germany, Spain, and Russia (such as Alexandra of Russia and her son Alexei shown here) came to have sons with hemophilia and daughters who were carriers.

The disease caused much heartbreak among the royalty. Kings and queens knew their sons might not live long. They might never grow up to become kings themselves. The parents did everything possible to protect their sons. They kept them from playing with pets. They would not let them run or climb trees. Life was not much fun for these boys. Some managed to escape all dangers and become adults. But many never made it beyond childhood.

There are now treatments available for people with hemophilia. Doctors can replace their platelets so that the blood can clot better. Doctors can also detect whether you carry the disease and can pass it on to your children.

CHAPTER FOUR

WHAT HAPPENS IN THE HEART?

The heart lies inside the chest, right between the lungs.

Its bottom points a little to the left. For this reason, many

people think the heart is on the left side of the chest.

The heart is the pump that sends blood out all through the body.

This organ is made of muscle tissue. The heart

muscle constantly squeezes and relaxes,

squeezes and relaxes. Each time it

does this, the heart is said to

beat. When the heart beats,

it pumps blood out into the

arteries. Later, blood returns to

the heart through the veins.

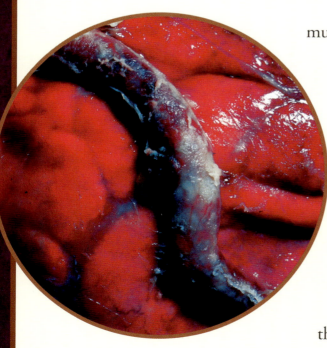

*Blood is pumped out of the heart through
arteries and into the heart through veins.*

When blood returns to the
heart, it first comes into the right
upper chamber. This is the right
atrium. Then the heart muscle
squeezes. This forces blood
through some flaps and down
into the right ventricle. The heart
muscle squeezes again, pushing
blood out into an artery. Blood
flows through this artery and into
the lungs.

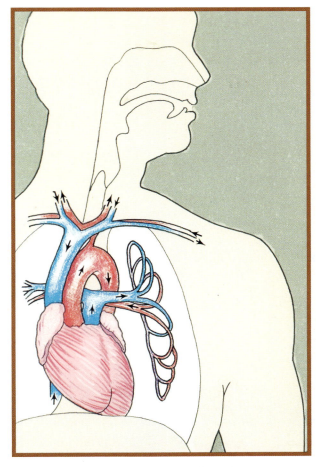

*The heart pumps blood out through arteries
to the lungs, found just beside the heart.
Veins bring blood from the lungs back into
the heart through the left atrium.*

Next, it leaves the lungs and comes back to the heart. This time,
it comes into the left upper chamber, or left atrium. Then the heart
beats again. Blood washes through another set of flaps and into the

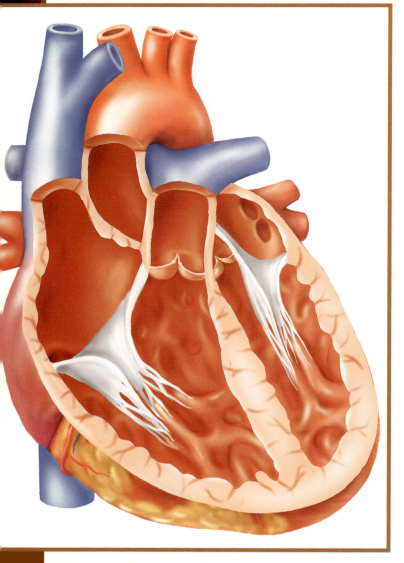

The heart pumps blood from the ventricles into arteries, shown in red. The blood circulates in the body and returns to the heart through veins, blue, that empty into the atria.

left ventricle. The heart muscle squeezes one more time. Blood then gushes into a large artery called the aorta (ay-OR-tuh). From there, it travels to every part of the body.

When blood comes into the heart, it always comes into an atrium. When it leaves the heart, it always leaves from a ventricle. Ventricles have very thick muscular walls. This is because they have the tough job of pushing blood out.

CHAPTER FIVE

WHERE DOES BLOOD GO NEXT?

When blood leaves the left ventricle, it first goes through the aorta. Many other arteries branch off from the aorta. Some of these arteries carry blood to the head. Some take blood to the arms and hands. Others carry blood to different organs.

Arteries split into smaller and smaller vessels. Blood flows into these smaller vessels and finally into capillaries. The walls of capillaries are quite thin. In fact, materials can actually move through these walls.

Capillaries are so small that blood cells just barely get through. But some very important things happen here. In the capillaries, blood really goes to work.

For one thing, the red cells let go of their oxygen. Other tissues in the area pick it up. All of the body's tissues need oxygen to work correctly. For example, muscles cannot move at all without oxygen. Hair and fingernails cannot grow without it. Eyes cannot see unless they get enough oxygen, and ears cannot hear. These body parts get oxygen from red blood cells passing through the capillaries.

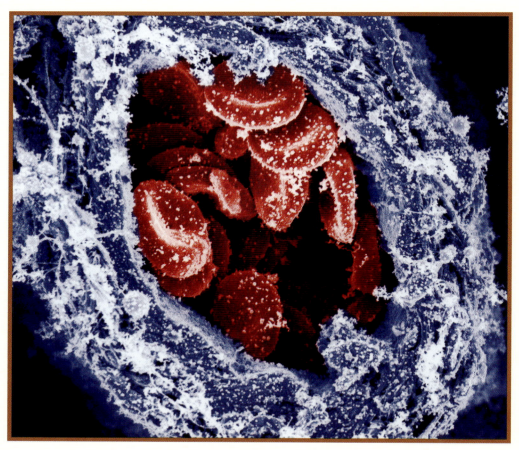

This digital picture shows red blood cells passing through a capillary in the ear.

Blood also brings nutrients to the tissues. Nutrients include such things as sugars, fats, and minerals. Some nutrients give tissues their energy. Others help tissues to build up and grow. Nutrients move through the capillary walls. Nearby tissues take them up and use them.

As the body's tissues work, they produce another gas. This is carbon dioxide. It is a waste material, and the tissues need to get rid of it. Carbon dioxide moves into the capillaries and into the blood. Other waste materials from the tissues also move in. The blood then carries it all away.

A lot happens as blood slowly moves through the capillaries. Oxygen moves out to the tissues. Nutrients move out as well. Carbon dioxide and other wastes move into the blood. Then blood moves from the capillaries into the veins. And the veins carry blood back to the heart.

CHAPTER SIX

WHAT HAPPENS IN THE LUNGS?

When blood gets back to the heart, it contains carbon dioxide. Blood next goes to the lungs for two very important reasons. In the lungs, it gets rid of the carbon dioxide. And it picks up more oxygen.

A colorized scan of the lungs taken through a powerful microscope shows the tiny air sacs.

The lungs are full of millions of tiny air **sacs.** Capillaries surround each of the sacs. These capillaries are just like the ones in the rest of the body. They are so tiny that blood cells move through in single file. The capillary walls are thin, and gases can move through easily.

24

Every time you exhale, carbon dioxide moves out of your lungs.

Each time you **inhale,** the air sacs fill up. Blood in the capillaries moves slowly past the sacs. Carbon dioxide moves out of the blood and into the air sacs. Oxygen moves from the air sacs and into the blood. Then you **exhale.** Carbon dioxide goes out with the breath. And oxygen-filled blood continues on to the heart.

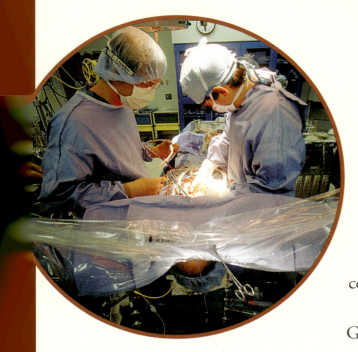

Doctors can sometimes perform surgery to fix heart problems and repair the circulatory system.

In an average day, a person inhales around 20,000 times. The heart beats more than 100,000 times. Billions of blood cells move through the capillaries. Gases come and go. But in some people, the circulatory system does not work properly. Often this is because they have heart problems.

Some children are born with a hole in the wall between the right and left chambers. Each time the heart beats, blood from one side enters the other side. Blood from the left side could wash into the right instead of going out to the rest of the body. Then the right side has to pump this extra blood to the lungs. Over time, this hard work could make the heart wear out. However, small holes sometimes

Exercise and good eating habits help keep your circulatory system working properly now and for the rest of your life.

close up on their own. Surgery often takes care of the larger holes.

Adults sometimes have heart diseases, too. The best way to avoid any heart problems when you are grown up is to start eating healthy foods and exercising now. That way, your circulatory system can keep doing its amazing job.

Glossary

absorbed (ab-ZORBED) To absorb something is to soak it up.

elastic (i-LASS-tik) Something that is elastic is stretchy.

exhale (eks-HAYL) To exhale means to breathe out.

infection (in-FEK-shuhn) An infection is an illness that is caused by a germ or virus that has entered the body.

inhale (in-HAYL) To inhale means to breathe in.

nutrients (NOO-tree-uhnts) Nutrients are the things found in foods that are needed for life and health.

sacs (SAKS) A sac is a part that is shaped like a little bag or pocket.

Questions and Answers about the Circulatory System

How much blood does my body have? The human body has an average of 1.32 gallons (5 liters) of blood flowing through the circulatory system.

How can I find my pulse? The easiest place to find your pulse is on the inside of your wrist. Use your index finger or middle finger of the other hand to feel your wrist until you feel the beat of your pulse. Don't use your thumb because it has its own pulse!

What is a blood transfusion? A blood transfusion takes place when new blood is pumped into a patient's circulatory system. People in surgery or who have been in accidents and have lost a lot of blood often need blood transfusions. Many people donate blood every year. The blood is often stored separated into platelets, plasma, and red blood cells for different patients to receive when they need it.

Did You Know?

- The heart and large blood vessels have smaller blood vessels of their own. These smaller vessels carry blood into the walls of the larger structures.

- At one time, people believed that a person's heart produced all thoughts and ideas. Now we know that the brain does our thinking for us!

- Deep inside certain bones, there is a red, mushy material called marrow. This is where the body makes blood cells.

- Smaller animals have much faster heartbeats than larger ones. In flight, a hummingbird's heart beats more than 1,000 times each minute. A resting elephant's heart beats about 25 to 30 times a minute.

- Blood filled with oxygen is bright red. Blood that has given up its oxygen is dark, brick red.

How to Learn More about the Circulatory System

At the Library

Brynie, Faith Hickman.
101 Questions about Blood and Circulation: With Answers Straight from the Heart.
Brookfield, Conn.: Twenty-First Century Books, 2001.

Stille, Darlene R.
The Circulatory System.
Danbury, Conn.: Children's Press, 1997.

Walker, Pam, and Elaine Wood.
The Circulatory System.
San Diego: Lucent Books, 2003.

On the Web

Visit our home page for lots of links about the circulatory system:
http://www.childsworld.com/links.html
Note to Parents, Teachers, and Librarians: We routinely verify
our Web links to make sure they're safe, active sites—
so encourage your readers to check them out!

Through the Mail or by Phone

THE AMERICAN HEART ASSOCIATION
NATIONAL CENTER
7272 Greenville Avenue
Dallas, TX 75231
800-242-8721
http://www.americanheart.org

AMERICAN STROKE ASSOCIATION
NATIONAL CENTER
7272 Greenville Avenue
Dallas, TX 75231
888-478-7653

NATIONAL HEART, LUNG, AND BLOOD INSTITUTE
NHLBI Health Information Center
Attention: Web Site
P.O. Box 30105
Bethesda, MD 20824-0105
301-592-8573
http://www.nhlbi.nih.gov

NATIONAL INSTITUTE OF
NEUROLOGICAL DISORDERS AND STROKE
National Institutes of Health
NIH Neurological Institute
P.O. Box 5801
Bethesda, MD 20824
800-352-9424
http://www.ninds.nin.gov

Index

About the Author

Susan H. Gray has a bachelor's and a master's degree in zoology, and has taught college-level anatomy and physiology courses. In her 25 years as an author, she has written many medical articles, grant proposals, and children's books. Ms. Gray enjoys gardening, traveling, and playing the piano and organ. She has traveled twice to the Russian Far East to give organ workshops to church musicians. She also works extensively with American and Russian friends to develop medical and social service programs for Vladivostok, Russia. Ms. Gray and her husband, Michael, live in Cabot, Arkansas.